PERIODICAL NOTES

ON THE

GERMAN ARMY

No. 36

HANDLING AND FIGHTING
OF THE
GERMAN TANK REGIMENT
AND
TANK BATTALION

Prepared by the
GENERAL STAFF(M.I.14), THE WAR OFFICE

10th October, 1941.

Published by

The Naval & Military Press Ltd

Unit 5 Riverside, Brambleside
Bellbrook Industrial Estate
Uckfield, East Sussex
TN22 1QQ England

Tel: +44 (0)1825 749494

www.naval-military-press.com
www.nmarchive.com

HANDLING AND FIGHTING OF THE TANK REGIMENT AND TANK BATTALION.*

CONTENTS

DISTRIBUTION

---

* Translated from a recently captured German document. These are provisional instructions valid pending publication of the Final Instructions for the Handling and Fighting of the Tank Regiment and Tank Battalion.

HANDLING AND FIGHTING OF THE TANK REGIMENT AND TANK BATTALION

I. CHARACTERISTICS AND ORGANIZATION

1. *The tank regiment.* Owing to its great fire power, its armour and its mobility the tank regiment forms the main driving force of the armoured division. Its strength lies in its ability to launch merciless surprise attacks in close formation. Enthusiastic and skilful leadership and boldness in employing this powerful assault weapon in the decisive sector ensure success. The other arms support the regiment in the execution of its fighting task. As a rule it fights· as an integral part of the armoured brigade.*

2. The tank regiment consists of :
    regimental headquarters with signal section and light tank troop ;
    two tank battalions† ;
    one regimental workshop company.

3. *The tank battalion* usually goes into action as an integral part of the tank regiment. Each tank battalion is equipped with the same number of tanks and weapons.

4. The tank battalion consists of :
    battalion headquarters ;
    headquarter squadron with signal section, reconnaissance section, light tank troop, pioneer section, and A.A. section ;
    two or three light tank squadrons†† ;
    one medium tank squadron ;
    one light tank column.

II. COMMAND

5. Daring and initiative are essential in commanding a tank unit. Commanders carry their troops to victory by their personal example. Careful study of the ground from maps must precede action. Air photographs can provide useful data for appreciation of the terrain over which the attack is to be made.

6. The element of surprise must be assured by constant and careful camouflage and by speed of movement.

7. Units must be held together for united and simultaneous action. Dispersal of forces must be avoided.

---

* If there is only one tank regiment in the division it comes directly under divisional orders.
† Note.—The present organization of a tank regiment is three mixed tank battalions.
†† These instructions are based upon the organization of battalions with three light tank squadrons.

8. The regimental commander will inform battalion commanders as early as possible about the situation, ground and plan so as to enable them to act in accordance with his instructions even if the situation should suddenly change.

9. The battalion commander will notify the squadron commanders as to his intentions in time for them to acquaint their units with their respective tasks. As a rule this will be done through verbal orders.

10. Under normal conditions orders within the regiment are transmitted chiefly by wireless. During tactical moves, however, wireless silence will usually be observed, and will only be broken immediately before going into action. Orders will accordingly be transmitted for as long as possible by D.R. Telephone communication can be used in camp and in the assembly area.

III. ON THE MARCH

11. On good roads with no traffic tracked vehicles can travel at a speed of 12 m.p.h. by day and 7 m.p.h. by night.

12. (*Omitted*).

13. Always endeavour to separate tracked vehicles from wheeled vehicles. This saves wear and helps to maintain the continuity of the march.

The only wheeled vehicles remaining with tracked vehicles are those required for the staff, the intercommunication, maintenance (T) and medical (S) services, the most essential fuel and supply vehicles of the A echelon battle transport, and part of the recovery section of the tank workshop company.

14. Marching orders must contain information about the enemy, our own intentions, the objective, the route to be followed, reconnaissance on the march, protection, time of departure, order of march (including allocation of transport columns, maintenance and medical services), the point at which the battalion or unit joins the column (*Einfädelungspunkte*), halts, position of the commander and special instructions regarding intercommunication. When marching by night the scale of illumination (*Beleuchtungstufe*) as ordered by the divisional commander must be given.

When issuing orders remember that owing to the considerable area usually covered by a division there is very often over an hour's delay between the time of issue and the first move. Warning orders giving the probable starting time and direction of march or the time and point of assembly are often advisable.

A good commander will see that formations and units take up the positions assigned to them in the column of march without unduly interrupting movement and without interfering with the movement of other formations or units.

Regiment

15. If the tank regiment forms a marching group within the division its commander is responsible for the speed and continuity of movement on the march, and also for the clearing of the roads at the time specified. Besides issuing orders for halts and rests, he is responsible for protection and camouflage, and for the refuelling and supply of the group.

2

If the marching group is moving independently he may also be responsible for reconnaissance, protection, and for marking the route.

When the regiment halts, units, as well camouflaged as possible, will keep close to the road so that they can resume the march at the shortest notice.

16. The engineers attached to the regiment will be placed well forward.

17. On the march intercommunication within the regiment is by D.R.

18. If the regiment has A.A. units at its disposal, arrangements must be made for their timely employment at vulnerable points, e.g. bridges and defiles.

19. If the regiment moves as advanced guard of the division it will normally throw out a screen including a light tank squadron as a point which may be as much as 15 minutes ahead. This point squadron is always accompanied by the attached engineers, and in most cases by medium tanks and part of the reconnaissance section of the foremost battalion.

Attached assault artillery marches behind the foremost battalion in the main column.

The regimental commander's position is between the advanced elements and the main column.

Battalion

20. If a tank battalion is moving independently along a road paras. 15-18 will apply.

21. If a tank battalion is employed as advanced guard, para. 19 will apply, the battalion commander moving with the point squadron.

22. If a tank battalion is located elsewhere in the column the battalion commander will usually move at the head of the battalion, followed by the H.Q. staff, the medium tank squadron and the light tank squadrons, A echelon battle transport and the remainder of the headquarter squadron.

23. The A.A. section of the battalion is generally distributed between the fighting echelon and the wheeled transport echelon so as to protect the latter from low level air attack.

IV. DEPLOYMENT

24. The opening of the battle is usually preceded by deployment. This makes the formation readier for action and reduces its depth. The formation taken up by the armoured unit will be that providing the most favourable conditions for action.

Orders for deployment are usually given by the senior commander. They may also be given by regimental or battalion commanders when they are in charge of the advanced guard or of an independent marching column.

If the armoured unit unexpectedly makes contact with the enemy or if it is forced to leave the road by enemy aircraft or artillery, it will be deployed on the orders of its commander or of the commander on the spot.

Double file or arrowhead formation will be taken up according to the ground.

If information about the enemy and orders already issued provide a sufficient guide to the best method of attack, inverted arrowhead formation may be adopted by the battalion in deploying. For the method of deployment *see* Appendix 1 (Formations and movements of the battalion).

Deployment is usually carried out on the move.

25. Close reconnaissance should be carried out immediately deployment is begun.

V. ACTION

A. The attack

26. The great offensive power of armoured troops produces its maximum effect when the tank regiment goes into action in close formation.

The tank battalion attacks independently,

    (*a*) as an advanced guard, in order to surprise the enemy whilst still unprepared, or in order to occupy points which are important for the further conduct of the battle ;

    (*b*) on the move, when it has been ordered to wait for other armoured units behind it to form up ;

    (*c*) when it has an independent task.

Battle order

Regiment

27. The tank regiment may attack with the two battalions in two successive waves or with both in line.*

If the regiment is fighting as part of the armoured brigade, the brigade decides the battle order.

28. The attack in waves enables the weight of the first blow to be maintained by the squadrons of the second wave, and thus makes possible a battle in depth.

Formation in depth is the best means of protecting the flanks of a regiment fighting within the enemy's zone of resistance.

The attack in waves facilitates control of the regiment and this formation should be the rule.

29. Action with two battalions in line and in little depth may be expedient when pursuing an already weakened enemy, or in withdrawal, when counter-attacking a pursuing enemy.

30. When battalions are attacking in line, and the regimental commander wishes to concentrate his forces towards the centre, he orders " central line."

31. The regimental commander moves in front of his regiment until he has ascertained that the first wave has attacked in the direction ordered. He then takes up a position sufficiently advanced to give him a good view of the action of the first wave and to allow him to control that of the second wave.

Battalion

32. Before the attack, the tank battalion deploys into several lines, the composition of which depends upon the enemy's position, the task in hand,

---

* If the regiment has three battalions the third battalion can be employed in reserve.

the lateral space available, the field of view and the position of the battalion in the battle order of the regiment.

As a rule two light tank squadrons constitute the first line, the medium tank squadron usually fighting in the second line in order to provide covering fire for the light tank squadrons. The third light tank squadron follows in the third line either to the rear of the exposed flank or along the axis of attack.

33. Endeavour to bring up the medium tank squadron in close formation for providing covering fire. Necessary conditions for this are :
    A clear view of the ground.
    Elevated fire position or gaps in the forward tank squadrons and a reasonable frontage of attack for the battalion (not more than 1,300 yards).
A poor field of view may necessitate the allocation of troops or half troops from the medium tank squadron to the light tank squadrons.

34. If an advance along a particular axis in successive waves is ordered by the regimental commander, the direction of attack within the battalion will be determined by (the movement of) the first line squadron. If the regimental commander has ordered a sector to be attacked by the battalion the latter can concentrate along an axis of its own choosing.

35. The battalion commander moves at the head of the battalion until he has ascertained that the battalion has taken up the correct direction and frontage for the attack. He then places himself sufficiently far forward to obtain a good view of the battle field and to control the rear squadrons. Similarly, the commander of the second wave must, if the ground permits, be in a position to observe the action of the rearmost elements of the first wave.

36. Orders for attack must give information about the enemy, situation of unit concerned and adjacent units, intention of the regimental or battalion commander, objective, battle order of the regiment or battalion, instructions regarding waves (for squadrons), co-operation with other arms, direction, line of attack, instructions for H.Q. units, maintenance and medical services, battle transport (if battalion, only inclusive of A echelon) and wheeled vehicles, intercommunication, position of commander.

Attack on the move

37. When attacking on the move it is essential to strike the enemy a swift and unexpected blow without dispersing one's own forces.

38. In order to take up battle order a halt for forming up is usually necessary. This must be carried out under the best possible cover from enemy observation and fire, and as quickly as possible in order to leave the enemy no time to get his A.Tk. weapons into position. The readier the unit is during the early deployment the shorter the halt necessary for forming up.

39. Unexpected encounters with the enemy or difficult terrain (for example, fighting one's way out of a defile) may necessitate attack from column of route or from narrow battle formation. Battle order must be taken up as soon as the leading tanks have gained sufficient space for the deployment of the succeeding tanks and the situation of the enemy and ground conditions allow.

Regiment

40. Close reconnaissance by the regimental H.Q. light tank troop should provide the regimental commander with the necessary information for drawing up his plan of action and choosing the battle formation to be adopted by the regiment. In particular the suitability of the ground for tank attack, and the locations of A.F.V. blocks and obstacles must be ascertained by thorough reconnaissance.

If both flanks of the regiment are exposed, battalions must be given orders as to which flank they are to reconnoitre.

Efforts must be made early to establish liaison with the arms supporting or accompanying the regiment in its attack.

41. When attacking on the move the regiment usually brings up its battalions in line. In this case it is the task of the first wave to smash the enemy and penetrate as deeply as possible.

The second wave is brought up in such a way that it can go into action in depth. Objectives will often only become apparent during the course of the action.

42. Close liaison with the commander of the divisional artillery is of particular importance since, when attacking on the move, little information will be available about the enemy before launching the attack and there will usually be little time for a verbal exchange of views. Where the artillery commander does not accompany the O.C. tank regiment in the command tank, liaison will be maintained by the artillery liaison party.

The artillery commander must know the orders for attack, the frontage, the axis of attack and the objective.

He must expect to receive constant requests for assistance against objectives which the regiment cannot engage with its own weapons.

43. The pioneer section and the attached elements from the divisional engineer battalion often form part of the first wave.

44. Reports of the objectives reached by the regiment are to be forwarded immediately by the commander to the higher formation.

Battalion

45. As soon as the battalion commander receives the order for attack he will bring the H.Q. light tank troop to the front or to the exposed flank of the battalion to assist the regiment in carrying out close reconnaissance. It may be necessary to reinforce the light tank troop with tanks from the battalion's light squadrons.

46. When attacking on the move the battalion will usually adopt inverted arrowhead formation.

47. Covering fire must always be arranged for the continued advance of the tank squadrons, the medium tank squadron being brought up for this purpose from sector to sector. The first and second waves must never lose touch.

48. In the attack the artillery commander and observer will accompany the foremost elements in their armoured command vehicle and will, at the request of the battalion commander, direct artillery fire chiefly against such enemy weapons as have not been dealt with by the tank weapons of the battalion. If, in exceptional cases, a battery of artillery has to co-operate with a tank battalion, fire control will also be exercised by the artillery liaison party.

Attack from the assembly point

49. Before moving up to the assembly point the approach roads and assembly point must be reconnoitred. They must provide cover from enemy ground and air observation. The assembly point should, if possible, always be within reach of the wheeled vehicles of B echelon.

50. At the assembly point the regiment is drawn up in battle formation as far as space and ground conditions permit, and prepares for action.

51. All preparations necessary for the attack must be made beforehand. These include :—

Thorough reconnaissance of the ground over which the attack is to be made.

Removal of blocks and obstacles in front of the main enemy battle position.

Acquisition of all information necessary for the attack by means of close reconnaissance.

Establishment of liaison with the commanders of supporting and accompanying arms.*

Establishment of liaison with the commanders of formations and units already in contact with the enemy in the area of attack.

Under certain circumstances, establishment of liaison with the commanders of infantry and lorried infantry formations attacking ahead of the armoured formations.

The results of reconnaissance by all arms of located enemy centres of resistance, especially of A.Tk. weapons and artillery, must be fully utilized.

52. Squadron commanders and as many subordinate commanders as possible should be given a detailed " picture " of the ground over which the attack is to take place, provided that this does not give away the intention to attack.

53. Wireless silence will be observed at the point of assembly so that the enemy receives no warning of the impending attack through increased wireless activity.

54. The armoured formation should move off from the assembly point in battle order. If the terrain does not permit this, a short halt for forming up after leaving the assembly point will be required.

Regiment

55. If the regiment attacks in several waves, the orders of the first wave will usually be to penetrate deeply with all speed into the main enemy battle position and to destroy the enemy's artillery.

The second wave, which follows immediately behind the first, will overpower those enemy infantry and heavy weapons which have not already been subdued by the first wave. In simultaneous attacks with infantry or lorried infantry the second wave enables the latter to follow up quickly and to exploit success.

---

* Engineers, M.G. and assault gun units.

56. If the regiment is ordered to assist the attack of infantry or of lorried infantry the commander of the tank regiment will be responsible. for keeping touch between his regiment and the lorried infantry. As a normal rule tank elements up to the strength of a light tank squadron are detailed by the regiment for direct co-operation with the lorried infantry.

57. The regimental commander may detail the second wave to bring up its medium tank squadron to reinforce the covering fire required for penetration by the first wave. In such a case this squadron would not usually be attached to the first wave.

58. Once penetration has been achieved the assault must immediately be carried deep into the main enemy battle position. This is the quickest and most certain means of breaking the enemy's resistance.

59. If elements of the A.Tk. battalion are attached to the tank regiment they are formed up in several waves immediately to the rear of the first wave in order to assist in overpowering the enemy's A.Tk. weapons during penetration. After penetration they are usually brought up behind the exposed flank of the first wave to support the latter in dealing with enemy tanks and also to cover the flank of the regiment.

60. Close co-operation with the engineers accompanying the tank attack is essential in order to ensure speedy removal of all A.F.V. blocks and obstacles which might prevent penetration into the main enemy battle position. The engineers may require protection by tanks whilst removing the obstacles.

Battalion

61. When attacking in waves the battalion composing the first wave will, provided it is not dealing with enemy A.Tk. weapons, also engage located enemy heavy weapons and centres of resistance ; but this must not interfere with the execution of the main task.

After reaching the objective of the attack, the commander must immediately organize the battalion to take up the necessary battle formation for further action. The battalion must always be ready to meet enemy counter attacks.

62. In the second wave the medium tank squadron supporting the first wave must be kept well up with the latter, so that it can provide the light tank squadrons with covering fire against such A.Tk. weapons as have not been located or overpowered by the first wave. The light tank squadrons (of the second wave) must seek out and destroy any enemy not dealt with by the light tanks of the first wave.

One of the main tasks of the second wave will be to repel enemy counter-attacks directed against the tank attack and the infantry (lorried) which follows it. To this end arrangements should be made when forming-up the second wave (after penetration) for the weight of the medium tank squadron to be used at the decisive point.

63. When penetration has been effected it is important that close reconnaissance, especially on the exposed flank, should be immediately resumed.

Repulsing close range attacks

64. Close range attacks must be expected when penetrating the main battle position and also in built-up areas or forests, particularly when the

enemy shows a strong will to resist. Such attacks will generally be made with Molotoff cocktails (petrol bombs).

The danger of close range attacks is increased when the speed of the tanks is reduced owing to enemy resistance, ground conditions, limited visibility, and when they are halted by ground obstacles. When tanks are compelled to slow down or halt they must arrange with one another for close range reconnaissance and mutual fire protection of their front, flanks and rear. Only by so doing will it be possible to shake off and destroy the enemy, who is usually well concealed and will only attack from very close quarters, taking advantage of dead ground which gives him concealment from the fire and view of the individual tanks.

Tank v. tank action

65. The decisive factors in tank v. tank action are :

Lightning appreciation of the situation and ground, and immediate action by leaders of every rank.

Timely realization of the strength and direction of the enemy tank attack.

Knowledge of the mechanical and fighting characteristics of the enemy's tanks.

66. Immediately the enemy tanks appear they must be attacked and destroyed with all available A.Tk. weapons, even if this should entail abandoning the original task. The more rapidly action is taken, the sooner will the armoured enemy be destroyed, and the sooner can the original task be resumed.

67. The enemy flank must be located as early as possible by close reconnaissance.

68. For the destruction of an armoured enemy, it is essential that there should be united action by all forces. It is essential that a strong fire front should quickly be formed so that the enemy can be surprised by fire and compelled to halt in his attack. This will prepare the way for the action of the rear waves. Whether the front, flank or rear of the enemy armoured force is to be attacked will depend on one's own strength, the ground and the weather.

Always try to fight against the wind with the sun behind, and engage the front of the enemy tanks so that they expose their vulnerable flanks to the regiment carrying out the counter attack. If the action is carried out in waves the regimental commander will order the first wave to make the frontal attack while the second wave, taking advantage of any favourable ground, will be thrown forward at full speed to deal the annihilating blow to the flank and rear of the enemy.

69. A.Tk. guns on S.P. mountings accompany the tank attack. Concentrated fire from the divisional artillery supports the action of the armoured formation.

70. In order quickly to avoid the aimed fire of enemy tanks appearing unexpectedly, to gain time for the establishment of a fire front, and to conceal the movements of the rear waves and lines, it may be advisable to put down a smoke screen between the enemy and one's own tanks.

71. If a tank battalion is unexpectedly attacked by enemy tanks the companies will begin by repulsing the attack independently. The battalion commander will endeavour to resume control of his battalion as quickly as possible.

9

72. If enemy tanks attempt evasive action they must be mercilessly pursued. Increase of speed to the very limit will be necessary to outflank the enemy tanks and to cut them off from their line of retreat. In this case co-operation with reconnaissance aircraft will be increasingly important.

Attacks across rivers

73. The tasks of the tank regiment when attacking across a river are :
to clear the near bank of enemy forces ;
to provide fire cover for moving up the bridging material and forming up the assault party (*Übersetztrupp*) ;
to support the assault party by engaging enemy points of resistance and by subsequently extending the bridgehead gained by the assault party.

74. Covering fire in making a crossing or attacking across a river is usually provided by the medium squadrons from concealed and frequently changed firing positions.

75. Tank battalions or units detailed to mop up the approaches will in the event of enemy air or artillery attacks take up a widely extended formation so that they do not interfere with the movements of the assault units and of the bridging column (engineers). Tank units not so employed are kept well back usually behind the starting line (*Ablauflinie*) laid down by the division.

76. After the attacking infantry have gained a small bridghead it will often be necessary to ferry over tank units with A.Tk. weapons as rapidly as possible in order to extend the bridghead or help in maintaining it.
The first elements of the tank units brought across will usually have to support the infantry fighting on the far bank.

77. If the regiment has to attack immediately after crossing the bridge, the regimental commander and the commander of the foremost battalion must obtain without delay a picture of the ground over which the attack is to be made. They will cross to the far bank in their armoured command vehicles, if possible before the bridging operations are completed. The light tank troops will cross with the leading elements of the regiment so that they can immediately be detailed for close reconnaissance. Of the units of the leading battalion the medium tank squadron will be the first to cross.

78. Assembly of the regiment after the necessarily protracted crossing of the bridge will take a considerable time. Hence at least the first battalion to cross must be assembled as soon as possible in order to avoid going into action in sections. If the bridgehead is small it may be necessary for the first units over, after a short halt for forming up, to attack in order to gain sufficient ground for the battalion to assemble.

Attack on a position with fixed defences

79. The bulk of the tank regiment is held back, if possible under cover from enemy fire from the fixed defences, until gaps have been made in the A.Tk. obstacles.
Close touch with the engineers who remove A.F.V. blocks and obstacles must be maintained.

80. The armoured formation will need covering fire most when passing through the gaps in the A.Tk. defences and while subsequently forming up in battle order in the enemy main battle position. Screening of the flanks with smoke may be expedient.

The objective of the tank attack is the enemy's artillery.

The most important object of close reconnaissance is to prevent the armoured formation from meeting with unexpected obstacles, particularly mines, inside the main battle position. The divisional engineers must be well forward in order to locate and remove such obstacles.

81. Part of the armoured formation, in particular the medium tank squadron, supports the unit which is to penetrate the main enemy battle position by engaging enemy centres of resistance in the intermediate zone (battle outposts), if possible from concealed fire positions.

B. The pursuit

82. Once the enemy gives way his formations must be broken up and annihilated by unremitting pursuit, even into the night. Only lack of fuel and ammunition can be allowed to halt the pursuit, and then only temporarily.

Personal example on the part of commanders is all-important.

83. Battle groups are often formed to carry out the pursuit on a wide front or to permit the use of detachments in such a way as to overtake the enemy in his retreat.*

In the pursuit, the tank battalion moves in broad arrowhead formation, and, if possible, in advance of the other arms.

84. It is important that touch be maintained in the pursuit. Medium tanks are usually attached to the light tank squadrons for this purpose. Any enemy resistance or counter attack must be immediately crushed by concentration of the battalion against the objective. Should enemy resistance increase, the regimental commander must endeavour to bring his unit to the attack in close formation.

85. In the pursuit particular attention must be given to the maintenance of intercommunication. Frequent reports on points reached and on the location of the defeated enemy forces will be passed back to superior commanders.

86. If the pursuit is continued into the night, pursuit groups will usually be formed to operate along the roads. Forces must keep close together. Advances by bounds may be advisable.

87. If darkness causes a halt in the pursuit, formations will if possible halt in country lending itself to A.Tk. defence. Armoured divisions when harboured must be disposed so as to bring uninterrupted fire to bear in all directions (hedgehog formation). Vehicles must be formed up with gaps between them in order to avoid major casualties in case of enemy bombing or raids. Wheeled vehicles and lightly armoured vehicles will be placed in the middle.

The covering party will consist of advanced reconnaissance sections on foot, who will call for prompt defensive fire from the tanks by means of prearranged signals.

---

* i.e. to reach important points, e.g. bridges, in the enemy's rear.

C. The defence

88. If, having reached the objective of the attack, the tank regiment has to defend ground gained until relieved by other arms, the bulk of the tanks will be held in reserve until the enemy attack begins. These tanks will be protected from enemy artillery and aircraft by dispersion and by the use of covered positions.

89. The armoured formation must protect itself against enemy surprise attacks by careful close reconnaissance, particularly in country with limited visibility. For this it may be necessary to reinforce the light tank troops.

90. Enemy reconnaissance may be hindered by the fire of individual tanks with long range weapons. These tanks should frequently change position.

91. If the enemy attacks he may be kept at bay by prompt, concentrated fire from the tanks. The armoured formations or units in reserve will be brought up to counter-attack in the most favourable direction, if possible against the enemy's flank.

92. In the event of an attack by enemy tanks the battle will be conducted according to paras. 65-72.

D. Breaking off the action

93. If the armoured formation has to break off action against a non-armoured enemy, it will withdraw under cover of the medium tank squadrons, supported by the fire of the divisional artillery. Once the light tank squadrons are outside the range of the enemy's A.Tk. weapons the medium tank squadrons will also retire by bounds.
Engineers will prevent pursuit by motorised enemy forces by blocking roads and tracks.

94. If the armoured formation is called upon to assist our own non-armoured forces to disengage it must repeatedly attack the pursuing enemy at close quarters, and from unexpected directions, until our own troops have withdrawn to a safe distance from the enemy. Such attacks are normally carried out on a wide front.

95. Breaking-off action against superior enemy armoured forces is facilitated by strong covering fire from the rear and, where possible, by operating from a tank-proof position.
Active reconnaissance to the flanks and the timely detailing of forces, particularly of attached A.Tk. troops and engineers, for flank protection, are necessary to prevent outflanking pursuit by armoured enemy forces.
If it is not possible to shake off the pursuit, the retreating armoured formation must take advantage of the ground and of any opportunities that present themselves to attack individual elements of the pursuing enemy with superior forces.

96. Artificial smoke screens facilitate disengagement and conceal the direction of withdrawal.

E. Action under special conditions

Action in fog

97. In fog, armoured units should be formed up on a narrow front and in depth. The form of deployment is usually double column.* Intervals and distances are reduced sufficiently for one tank to be visible to its neighbour.

98. It will usually prove of advantage to move the unit or formation by bounds. In order not to lose direction the deployed formation will, if possible, keep to tracks and clearly visible ground leading in the direction of the objective. The compass bearing of the general direction of the attack is given by the battalion to units.

99. In order to avoid sudden encounters with enemy A.Tk. weapons, obstacles, and blocks, and to guard against the danger of close range attacks (particularly in the case of sudden breaks in the fog), close reconnaissance and observation are of particular importance. Motor cyclist troops will normally maintain communication between formations and will be responsible for immediate covering and reconnaissance duties. When the fog clears distances and intervals must quickly be increased.

Action in built-up areas and in woods

100. If the armoured formation is compelled to fight in built-up areas and woods, the attack will be directed to outflanking the rear or deep flank of the enemy. In front the enemy must be pinned down, his centres of resistance being held or blinded with smoke. The burning of houses will hasten success. Close liaison between the units making the frontal attack and those executing the outflanking movement is essential.
Large inhabited areas and woods must be captured piecemeal and mopped up by sectors.

101. When combing through larger woods, the battalion will adopt a narrow, deep formation. For this purpose medium tank troops are usually attached to light tank squadrons.

102. The danger of a sudden enemy attack from close quarters must be met by increased reconnaissance and covering fire from tank to tank. Reconnaissance, observation and covering fire to the front, flank and rear by light tank elements are therefore of particular importance.

Action in mountainous country

103. Action in mountainous country requires extremely careful preliminary ground reconnaissance. If possible the armoured formation should follow the slopes and valleys so that the advance is not delayed by frequent crossing of gradients and gorges.

104. Steep slopes neutralize the effect of tank weapons. Covering fire therefore requires particular control where deep gorges have to be crossed.
Roads in defiles with precipitous sides, particularly in high mountains, afford no possibilities for the employment of armoured formations. Tanks can therefore only be used in small fighting groups amounting frequently to not more than a troop each. Armoured forces are therefore as a rule attached to lorried infantry or infantry formations.

* See Appendix 1.

VI. PROCEDURE WHEN ENCOUNTERING MINES

105. The high speed at which armoured formations move involves the risk of tanks unexpectedly striking enemy mines.

The longer the delay caused by encountering mines the more time will the enemy gain for strengthening his A.Tk. defences and for concentrating on important points.

106. Should, therefore, enemy mines and, in particular, minefields be expected in the sector in which the armoured formation is to attack, the principal task of the light tank troops detailed for observation and reconnaissance will be to identify the position and size of the enemy's minefields in time and to forward an early report. It will be expedient to attach engineer sections as scouts to the light tank troops reconnoitring to the front.

107. The engineers attached to the tank regiment will always be well forward in the first wave and will accompany the leading armoured unit in order quickly to remove mines or clear lanes through the minefield.

108. When it is necessary to cross mine-strewn ground it may be advantageous to disperse formations in width and depth. In the leading waves the tanks of the second and third line will follow in the tracks of those in the first line. The same applies to the rear waves.

109. Minefields of major width and depth must be circumvented. For this it is necessary that observation and reconnaissance patrols be sent out in good time, that an early decision be reached and subsequent orders for detours be given. The regimental commander will decide whether the original battle formation will be retained whilst the minefield is being circumvented or whether the formation will have to be adapted to the enemy situation and to the ground. He will inform the senior commander of his decision and will re-establish the original battle formations as soon as the situation permits.

110. If the minefield cannot be circumvented the formation must halt and take cover. Close reconnaissance will be intensified in order to provide detailed information regarding the positions of the mines and the extent of the minefield.

111. First tasks will include a search for other openings for attack and the provision of covering fire for the engineers. The formation will be held ready to form up immediately lanes have been created or the minefield has been removed.

112. Commanders of all ranks must themselves immediately endeavour to discover gaps in the minefield or to employ their engineers in making lanes under the covering fire of the tanks.

113. Minefields are often only recognized after the foremost tanks have already struck the mines. When this happens the tanks in the minefields will be withdrawn and recovered under the covering fire of the rear units.

The battalion or regimental commander will be responsible for ordering the withdrawal of tanks which have entered the minefield and for ordering the halt and assembly of the formation.

114. Smoke screens emitted by the tanks themselves, or smoke shells fired by the tanks and artillery detailed for covering fire, are effective means of protection from enemy reconnaissance and fire when mines are encountered.

115. (*Omitted.*)

VII. HARBOURS

116. The great number of vehicles in a tank regiment usually necessitates harbours being made in several groups ; advantage should be taken of habitations in areas affording cover.

Harbours must be camouflaged from ground and air observation and must allow free movement in several directions (i.e. they must not be hemmed in).

117. If in exceptional cases the tank regiment has to provide its own protection for harbours against enemy land forces, elements of the light tank squadrons reinforced by tanks from the medium squadron will be employed so that

    (*a*) by day they completely cover with fire from high ground any area which the enemy might occupy ;

    (*b*) by night they are able to cover the approach roads with fire, whilst they themselves keep to roads and tracks.

118. Erection of obstacles by the pioneer section and the motor cyclist detachment is advisable.

119. Quick intercommunication between the covering troops and the resting troops must be assured.

120. Protection from enemy air attacks will be given by the A.A. sections attached to the battalions.

The battalion commander may order extra protection by the M.Gs. of the tank squadrons.

121. Although the tank regiment while in harbour may be standing by in readiness to move, roads and tracks passing through the harbour area must always be kept clear for the movements of other formations.

VIII. TRANSPORT, MAINTENANCE & MEDICAL SERVICES

Battalion

122. Battle transport is divided into A echelon battle transport (*Gefechtstross I*) and B echelon battle transport (*Gefechtstross II*).

A echelon battle transport must be kept small. Its composition is variable and must be adapted to operational requirements. The following may belong to A echelon battle transport.

    P.O.L. lorries ;
    Ammunition lorries ;
    Fitters' lorry for armourers ;
    Certain of the reserve crews ;
    Field kitchens.

123. During the march A echelon battle transport will remain in battle formation.

When deployment begins, it will follow in close formation under a single commander so that before the battalion goes into action such transport as is necessary can be brought up rapidly in order to relieve crews and to provide for maintenance.

124. All remaining vehicles of A echelon battle transport will move with B echelon. The latter will move in close formation with the regiment. Its movement is frequently controlled by the divisional commander.

125. The commanders of A and B battle transport echelons must be experienced and energetic officers.

126. During action the light aid detachments form part of the fighting units. Their duties are determined by the battalion commander.
The commander of the L.A.Ds.—the battalion technical officer—decides which vehicles will be sent to the Tank Workshop Company for repair. He acts as a link between the battalion commander and the regimental technical officer.

127. The ration vehicles of battalion headquarters and of the tank squadrons form part of the supply transport ; they are commanded by the battalion messing officer.

128. The baggage transport forms part of the battalion transport and moves with B echelon battle transport except when placed under the orders of the regimental or divisional commander.

129. The medical services are controlled by the battalion medical officer.
Rapid medical assistance, particularly in battle, must be provided by a medical officer, who will accompany the attack in an armoured ambulance.
The second medical officer is responsible for setting up the regimental aid post and for the evacuation of wounded to the main dressing station.

IX. SUPPLY

Regiment

130. The regimental commander must give particular attention to the task of maintaining his tanks ready for action. He has under his orders a workshop company for the repair of tanks.

131. The chief task of the tank workshop company is the repair of tanks. In order to work efficiently the tank workshop company must to a certain extent be stationary. Movement by bounds is therefore necessary if it is to work in one place for several days. Its timely and appropriate employment is of decisive importance in maintaining the fighting strength of the regiment.

132. Where the recovery section does not follow behind A echelon it must be brought up into position at an early opportunity.

Battalion

133. The battalion commander is responsible for the supply of his battalion.
Complete supply arrangements for the tank battalion must be made

before the battalion goes into action. Battle transport must be divided up in accordance with para. 122. On a march during which no action is anticipated, P.O.L. lorries and a number of the field kitchens will move with the tank squadrons. This will reduce the time required for refuelling and for serving meals at the end of the march.

134. On long marches additional fuel will be carried in the A.F.Vs. Refuelling will take place before going into action. The spare fuel carried by A.F.Vs. will be put into their tanks as soon as an encounter with the enemy seems likely. In order not to jeopardize the efficiency of fuel supply, empties must be taken back or, when movement is too rapid for this, dumped in an orderly manner. The location of the dump will be reported.

135. Fresh supplies must be issued to troops after, or during pauses in, an engagement. Rations, ammunition and fuel must be brought up, wounded attended to and tank recovery services organized. Fighting strength must be made up as rapidly as possible.

APPENDIX 1

FORMATIONS AND MOVEMENTS OF THE BATTALION

A.—Formations

1. Distinction is made between :

Drill Formations : " Battalion Column," " Line Ahead," " Double Line Ahead."

Marching Formations : " Line Ahead " (also marching order) and " Double Line Ahead."

Battle Formations : " Arrowhead " and " Inverted Arrowhead."

The intervals and distances given for these formations are only rough indications. Touch within the Battalion formation must never be lost.

2. Unless otherwise ordered, the right leading company is responsible for direction and approach.

3. It is only in drill formations that tanks of Battalion Headquarters need keep their places as shown below.

4. Battalion Column is the usual drill formation (*see* Fig. 1). The squadrons are in squadron columns.

5. Line ahead is the marching formation of the tank battalion on the road.

6. Arrowhead is a suitable formation for the battalion to move in when deployed (*see* Fig. 2). The frontage of the battalion in arrowhead formation is approximately 545 yards, and the depth approximately 1,960 yards.

FIG. I.
BATTALION COLUMN FORMATION.

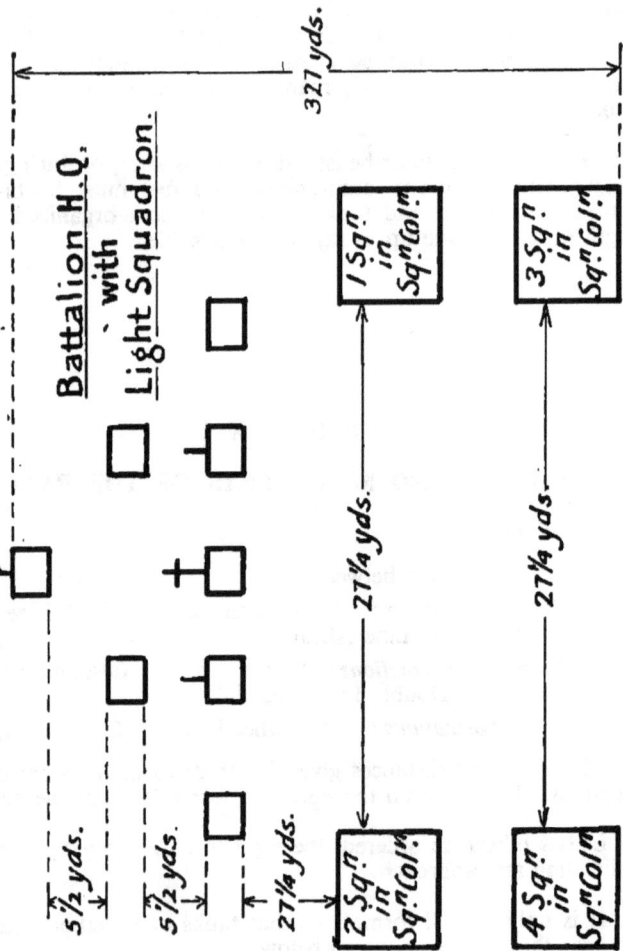

Battalion H.Q.
with
Light Squadron.

5½ yds.

5½ yds.

27¼ yds.

327 yds.

2 Sqⁿ
in
Sqⁿ Colⁿ.

27¼ yds.

1 Sqⁿ
in
Sqⁿ Colⁿ.

4 Sqⁿ
in
Sqⁿ Colⁿ.

27¼ yds.

3 Sqⁿ
in
Sqⁿ Colⁿ.

109 yds.

NOTE : Distances and intervals are only approximate.

18

FIG 2.

THE BATTALION IN ARROWHEAD FORMATION. ⊗

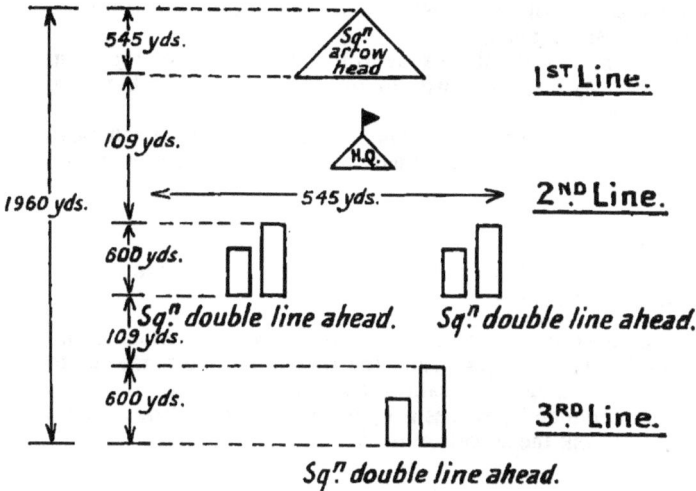

545 yds.

Sqⁿ arrow head

1ˢᵀ Line.

109 yds.

H.Q.

1960 yds.

545 yds.

2ⁿᴰ Line.

600 yds.

Sqⁿ double line ahead.   Sqⁿ double line ahead.

109 yds.

600 yds.

3ᴿᴰ Line.

Sqⁿ double line ahead.

⊗ Distances & intervals are only approximate.

FIG. 3.

THE BATTALION IN INVERTED ARROWHEAD FORMATION. ⊗

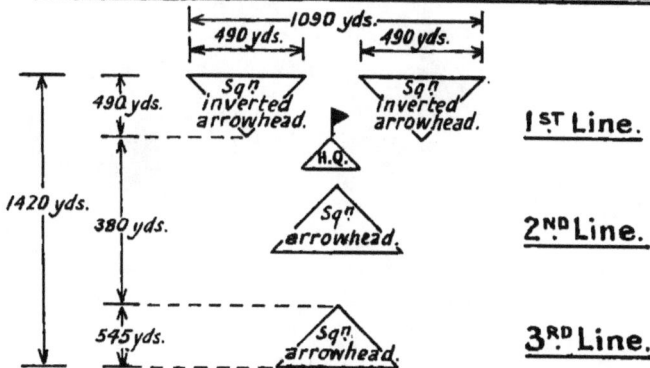

1090 yds.

490 yds.   490 yds.

490 yds.

Sqⁿ inverted arrowhead.   Sqⁿ inverted arrowhead.

1ˢᵀ Line.

H.Q.

1420 yds.

380 yds.

Sqⁿ arrowhead.

2ⁿᴰ Line.

545 yds.

Sqⁿ arrowhead.

3ᴿᴰ Line.

⊗ Distances & intervals are only approximate.

19

7. Inverted arrowhead is the most common formation for the battalion in attack (*see* Fig. 3). In this case the frontage of the battalion is about 1,090 yards, and the depth approx. 1,420 yards. The leading squadrons are also in inverted arrowhead formation.

8. Unless otherwise ordered the right-hand leading squadron gives the direction and is the pivot for all changes of formations. The rest march on it or deploy from it.

In arrowhead or inverted arrowhead the next squadron will usually move up on its right. When, in inverted arrowhead formation, it is required to move up left of the forward squadron, the order "Inverted arrowhead left" must be given.

In arrowhead formation the third squadron will move to the right ; in inverted arrowhead formation it will follow in the centre behind the first-wave squadrons.

In both arrowhead and inverted arrowhead, the last squadron will move in rear (*see* Figs. 2 and 3). Special orders must be given for any desired variations.

B.—Transmission of orders

9. The movements of the battalion will be directed by orders in wireless from the battalion commander.

10. The battalion commander issues orders by wireless either to all squadrons by collective messages (using the battalion code name) or to individual squadrons (using the squadron code name).

If the battalion commander wishes a squadron to acknowledge receipt of messages he must ask the squadron to do so.

C.—Wheeled vehicles

11. The formations for the wheeled vehicles of the battalion are those laid down in M.T. training instructions.

12. Unless employed for special purposes, the battalion's wheeled vehicles will usually move in one or more groups.

APPENDIX 2

MARCH TABLE, ROAD SPACING AND SPEED OF THE TANK BATTALION AND TANK REGIMENT

Unit	Extended at the Halt Yards*	10 m.p.h.		15 m.p.h.	
		Yards	Minutes	Yards	Minutes
Battalion Including B. Echelon Battle Transport.	1525	5515	20	8175	18
Battalion without B Echelon Battle Transport.	1090	4330	17	6320	13
Regiment Including B. Echelon Battle Transport.	3270	15260	45	18530	40
Without B. Echelon Battle Transport.	2400	9135	34	13625	30

* The length of Units when halting under war time conditions is the same as at 15 m.p.h.

Forming up times : (on favourable ground).

Battalion : From column of route to battalion inverted arrowhead
  10—15 min.

From battalion column to battalion inverted arrowhead
  5—10 min.

Regiment : From column of route to action in waves
  20—25 min.
  to action by flanks
  25—30 min.
  From battalion column
  10—15 min.

APPENDIX 3
SYSTEM OF MAP REFERENCES

In transmitting orders, forwarding reports and controlling artillery fire, use will be made of the following system of map references based on the line of thrust (*Stosslinie*).

Two points (if possible church spires) in the area of the division's advance will be given by divisional H.Q. and joined on the map by a line, called the line of thrust (*Stosslinie*), running approximately in the line upon which the division is to advance. The starting line is marked on the map, the point at which it intersects the line of thrust being the zero point.

From the point to be indicated a perpendicular is dropped to the line of thrust. The co-ordinates of this point are then obtained by measuring the distance on the map from the zero point to the point of intersection with the perpendicular and then the distance along the perpendicular from the line of thrust to the point to be indicated. Both distances are given in centimetres, the word *rechts* or *links* being inserted between them according to whether the point indicated lies right or left of the line of thrust facing the enemy.

For example, a point situated 9 cm. from the starting line and 2·7 cm. to the right of the line of thrust on the map will be referred to in wireless messages as " 9 right 2·7 ".

In order to make wireless interception by the enemy more difficult, divisional H.Q. will order, on different days, the zero point to be referred to not as zero but as some other number. Should the division change direction the point of departure from the original line of thrust will be given a new reference number, so making interception still more difficult.

DIAGRAM SHOWING SUPPLIES.

Ammunition, Fuel, Rations, Field post office.

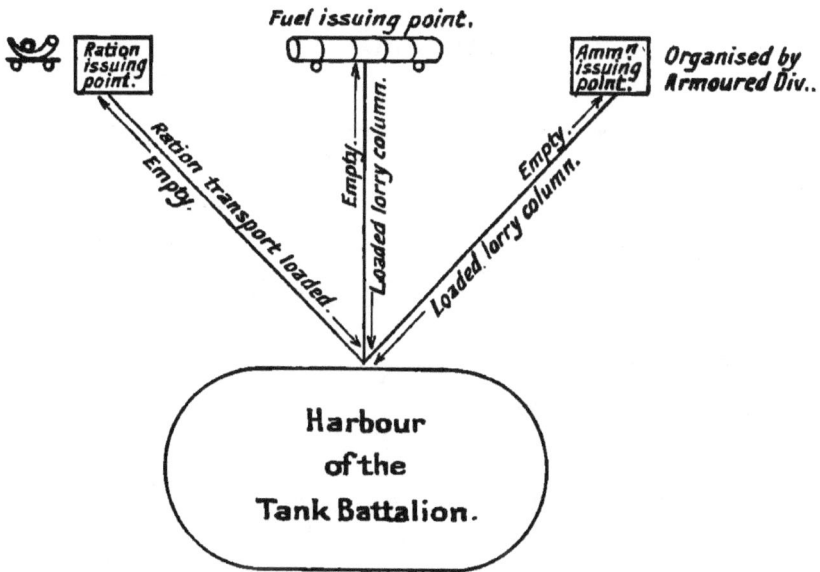

Fuel issuing point.

Ration issuing point.

Ammⁿ issuing point. Organised by Armoured Div..

Ration transport loaded.

Empty.

Empty. Loaded lorry column.

Empty. Loaded lorry column.

Harbour of the Tank Battalion.

"Empty" *transports take* :

    (a) 1ST Column ("A" echelon) :
       *to ammunition issuing point,
       empty boxes, dismantled
       (ausgebaute) parts and
       u.s. material.*

       *To fuel issuing point :
       empty containers.*

    (b) Ration transport :
       outgoing mail : empty boxes.

Diagram showing the
ALLOCATION OF THE MAINTENANCE SERVICES.
A.F.V's., M.T., Spare parts.

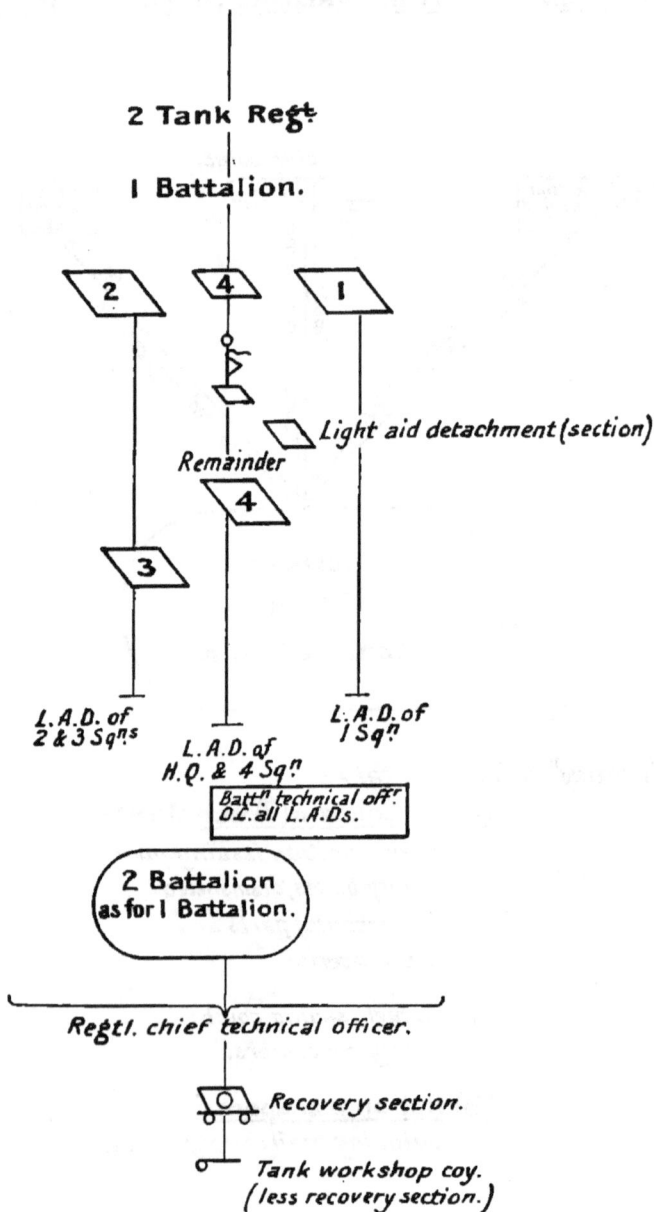

2 Tank Reg^t

I Battalion.

| 2 | | 4 | | I |

Light aid detachment (section)

Remainder

4

3

L.A.D. of
2 & 3 Sq^{ns}

L.A.D. of
H.Q. & 4 Sq^n

L.A.D. of
I Sq^n

Batt^n technical off^r.
O.C. all L.A.Ds.

2 Battalion
as for I Battalion.

Regtl. chief technical officer.

Recovery section.

Tank workshop coy.
(less recovery section.)

TRAINING MANUALS, TEXT BOOKS AND INSTRUCTIONS

The backbone of all successful armies is its training and tactics. The Naval and Military Press publishes many such manuals of instruction - all perviously long out of print . So, whether your interest lies in the infantry and cavalry tactics of the earliest regiments of the British army in the 18th century, or the weapons manuals and firing instructions of 20th century warfare, the Naval and Military Press has the right book for you.

www.naval-military-press.com

MINES AND BOOBY TRAPS 1943

This is a War Office pamphlet, issued mid-war, in 1943. Its purpose is to introduce sappers to mines commonly used by the British Army – and how to deal with similar devices set by the Germans. The devices described and illustrated cover British anti-tank; grenade; shrapnel and assorted booby trap switches. Enemy mines are covered in chapter 2 with anti-tank, Teller mine types; French anti-tank; Hungarian; anti-personnel German and Italian; and igniters.This is a concise but comprehensive guide for British Army sappers in the art of demining or mine clearance.

9781474539395

THE .303 LEWIS GUN

Illustrated with good clear line drawings this 1941 weapon guide tells the Home Guard Volunteer how to use the 303 Lewis Gun effectively against the invading enemy.A reprint of an original handbook for the .303 Lewis Gun, that was first published in 1941. This book is a practical guide to the handling and maintenance of this iconic weapon.In the crisis following the Fall of France, where a large part of the British Army's equipment had been lost up to and at Dunkirk, stocks of Lewis guns in both .303 and .30-06 were hurriedly pressed back into service, primarily for Home Guard use. Full of fascinating information, this book taught the user the guns capabilities and all he needed to know about maintenance and combat use. Number 2 in the wartime Nicholson & Watson "Know Your Weapons" series, that offer all the important information in a more vivid style than an official publication. Illustrated with good clear line drawings.

9781474539456

ANTI-TANK WEAPONS
Smash The Tank

An insight into the amateur side of World War 2. Diagrams illustrate the main points and the devices, such as the Thermos Bomb;Phosrhorus Bomb;Sticky Bombs; that could be cobbled together from household items are described.This pamphlet was available to the Home Guard and describes the German tank and how to destroy it. It is an early War publication c1940, dealing with the light tanks used by the Germans, also the author gives examples of anti-tank actions in the Spanish Civil War, in which he took part. I'ts is a fascinating look at the "enthusiastic" approach to killing tanks.

9781474539449

TANK HUNTING AND DESTRUCTION 1940

The stated object for the distributing of this War Office manual was as "A guide and help to troops who have the determination and nerve to destroy tanks at close quarters". Intended for fighting on home soil after the very real possibility of a full German invasion, "Operation Sea Lion", this is a remarkable if somewhat naive snap shot of Britain state of preparedness,in her most dangerous hour.

The contents details Tank hunting, Tank characteristics,Tactical action,Road blocks,ambushes Ect,also includes an interesting appendix on Molotov Cocktails, and materials on other ways to destroy tanks.

9781474539401

TROOP TRAINING FOR LIGHT TANK TROOPS NOVEMBER 1939

Very early War tactics pertaining to various aspects of training with and employing armour in the British Army. Covering in concise detail that which a Light tank crew needed to know to be effective in action.

In the early years of the war, Germany held the initiative. German forces used Blitzkrieg tactics in France in 1940, making full use of the speed and armour of tanks to break through enemy defences. It was clear that German tank tactics had evolved during the inter-war period. By contrast, Britain and the Allies were playing catch-up.

9781474539302

JAPANESE WEAPONS ILLUSTRATED
September 1944

This period 'Restricted' laced binding manual was intended to be an aid to the identification of Japanese Army equipment, with sections covering: Tanks, both two-man, Tankette, light and medium; Armoured Cars; Self-Propelled Guns; Anti-Tank Guns; Artillery; Anti-Aircraft Guns; Mortars & Grenade Dischargers; Small Arms; Flamethrowers etc. Produced one year before the surrender of Japan, this work gives a good overview of the weapons the allies would find, fighting an army that despite being on the back foot, was still capable of stiff resistance in an almost entirely defensive role..

9781474539432

NOTES ON THE GERMAN ARMY-WAR
December 1940

An early war 393-page 'Notes' periodical manual from December 1940. It is a detailed review, for use in the field. The manual looks at every aspect of the "Blitzkrieg" German Army (and, to some extent, the Air Force) and gives details as known at the time.

It covers the fighting arms and the services behind them – tactics, organisation, weapons and equipment. It usefully also includes a colour section on uniforms and insignia, a black-and-white plate section of small arms, infantry support and anti-tank weapons, artillery and AFVs. A series of pull-outs related to the text covering tanks etc. are also reproduced.

This is an important first-class picture of the complex fighting machine that was the German Army at the end of the campaigns of 1940, only six months before the invasion of Russia.

9781474539203

GERMAN MINES AND TRAPS

Mid-1940 War Office manual with details of German mines, both the Teller and S-mine (Bouncing Betty) are covered, with techniques for disarming. Good clear full-page line drawings give both practical and technical information. Highly recommended because of the illustrations, which show how these devices worked and the components.

9781474535809

NOTES ON ENEMY ARMY IDENTIFICATIONS ITALY
October 1941

This period handbook was published to give British military personnel a better understanding of the principal characteristics of both the Italian army and the Black Shirt Militia under active service conditions , it is dated October 1941.

It begins with a description of distinctive branches, or specialities, the most characteristic of which was the arm of the Royal Carabinieri, a semi-military body occupying, historically, the senior position in the Army. Other specialities included the Grenadiers of Sardinia, the Bersaglieri, the Alpini and the San Marco Marine Regiment

The handbook then goes on to show, in order, the organisation of Command and Staff, of formations (corps and divisions) and of the arms and services; services, supply and transportation; ranks, plates (many in colour) cover uniforms, insignia, medals and decorations; armament and equipment and a chapter on the Air Force, There are chapters on tactical doctrine and principles of employment, on permanent fortifications, camouflage and abbreviations. Finally there is a brief index.

9781474539746

MANUAL OF GUERILLA TACTICS
Specially Prepared And Based On Lessons From
The Spanish And Russian Campaigns

One of the excellent, concise Bernards Pocket Books, intended to show members of the Home Guard and the regular forces that war is not conducted in a gentlemanly way – it is kill or be killed.

9781474539463

THE OFFENSIVE OF SMALL UNITS
September 1916

This is a periodical tactical manual from 1916, it focuses on the manner in which the French organised and executed their attacks and counterattacks . Summarised from the French, it lays out the process by which to operate in attacks on the German trenches. Focused purely on the operation of infantry, the purpose of this British translation is to give small infantry units the benefit of the French experience in regard to the best methods of combat, in offensive operations.

9781474537971

TRENCH WARFARE
Notes on attack and defence, February 1915

This important period manual was published in early 1915 when hope of a quick ending to the war disappeared, and trench warfare had begun to dominate the Western Front.
The manual strives to instil an offensive spirit and gives practical examples on: Close quarter, local, methods of successful warfare, and German attacks. The salient points to gather were preparation and co-operation between artillery and infantry, and that the capture of trenches is easier than their retention. Two plates illustrating tactics complete this official publication.
9781474539807

Ministry Of Home Security
OBJECTS DROPPED FROM THE AIR 1941

An illustrated Official and confidential publication, covering the many and varied types of objects that were falling from principally German aircraft during the Second phase of the blitz, including high explosives,incendiary bombs and small arms ammunition. Complete with 8 page addendum.
9781783319541

THE MUSKETRY INSTRUCTIONS
FOR THE GERMAN INFANTRY 1887
(Schiessvorshrift fur die Infanterie)
Translated for the intelligence Division War Office

Translated for the War Office by Colonel C W Bowdler Bell

A facsimile that includes the supplement for the German Infantry for 1887. Musketry exercises were intended to give the infantry instruction in shooting, to make effective use of their firearm in battle. As such the manual shows important details designed to make the infantry soldier battle-ready by the end of his first year of service. Instruction is subdivided into Preparatory exercises; Target practice; Field firing; Instructional firing; Inspection in musketry; Proving the rifle M/61.84 and revolver M/83. Many black powder weapons were still used, mainly for training purposes, up to end of the First World War.
9781783313631

www.ingramcontent.com/pod-product-compliance
Lightning Source LLC
Chambersburg PA
CBHW071458070426
42452CB00040B/1862